The Sequence

by Bob Orsillo

THE SEQUENCE
BY BOB ORSILLO

The Sequence
by Bob Orsillo

Copyright © 2007 Bob Orsillo

First Edition

ISBN: 978-0-6151-7524-9
Library of Congress Control Number: 2007908808

For Donna with much love and respect.

The Forward

Art is a unique journey into the mind and emotions of each of us. No one person will look at an artistic expression with the same eye. What one might feel or see will be different from the next even if the subject portrayed is a simple and common item. For example viewing a vase of flowers might bring forth happy memories to one person, sad to another while someone else will reflect on the perfection of nature. When art is comprised of more complicated subjects, the thoughts explode into a dazzling display of ideas.

Bob Orsillo's Sequences takes you into your own individual adventure of provoking ideas.

Each owner of this book will discover their own vision which may change over

time as they experience life and the changes and growth within themselves.

So what you relate to today might be entirely different when you return once

again. You will encounter a new impression every time you open the cover. I

am always surprised with a new and thought provoking revelation with each

new glimpse into Bob Orsillo's world.

Leah Anne O'Bryan
Author / Historian

The first of the three Sequences presented in this book began in the late 1970's. The last was completed in 2006.

The Sequences selected for this book have been exhibited in the United States of America, England, Austria, Germany, Brazil, Venezuela, Cuba, Russia, New Zealand and Italy.

The Cats Eye Sequence is exhibited in the round whenever possible.
The Ghost Sequence is exhibited linear.
The Life Sequence is exhibited linear.

All three Sequences are in private collections. Each is exhibited on a regular basis.

Contents

The Sequence:

Art is a visual language. Art is a form of communication between people who may never meet and sometimes are hundreds if not thousands of miles or years apart. Art transcends time, brings ideas and passions from the past to the future. A single piece of art is a window to moments past. The Sequence takes those moments and ties them together into a conversation.

The Sequence is not new. In recent times Minor White made brilliant use of the sequence in black and white photography. But do not confuse this with frame by frame photography or a series of paintings on a specific subject.

Somewhat like the Fibonacci sequence in mathematics, each successive image is the sum of the two that precede it. Unlike the Fibonacci sequence, this happens naturally on an instinctual level without premeditation.

In its simplest form the Sequence is a group of individual thoughts standing on their own. When seen together the thoughts become conversation inviting you to join in. As is true in verbal conversation there is no incorrect response, the reason being each person enters the conversation from their own personal perspective bringing with them their own life experience to join together with the art, thus the sequence and the art become a personal experience for the individual.

The Sequence is collaboration between the artist and the viewer.

Bob Casilli

Fibonacci sequence

In mathematics, an infinite series in which each successive integer is the sum of the two that precede it—for example, 1, 1, 2, 3, 5, 8, 13, 21, 34…. In computing, Fibonacci numbers are used to speed binary searches by repeatedly dividing a set of data into groups in accordance with successively smaller pairs of numbers in the Fibonacci sequence. For example, a data set of 34 items would be divided into one group of 21 and another of 13. If the item being sought was in the group of 13, the group of 21 would be discarded, and the group of 13 would be divided into 5 and 8; the search would continue until the item was located. The ratio of two successive terms in the Fibonacci sequence converges on the Golden Ratio, a "magic number" that seems to represent the proportions of an ideal rectangle. The number describes many things, from the curve of a nautilus shell to the proportions of playing cards or, intentionally, the Parthenon, in Athens, Greece.

GHOST

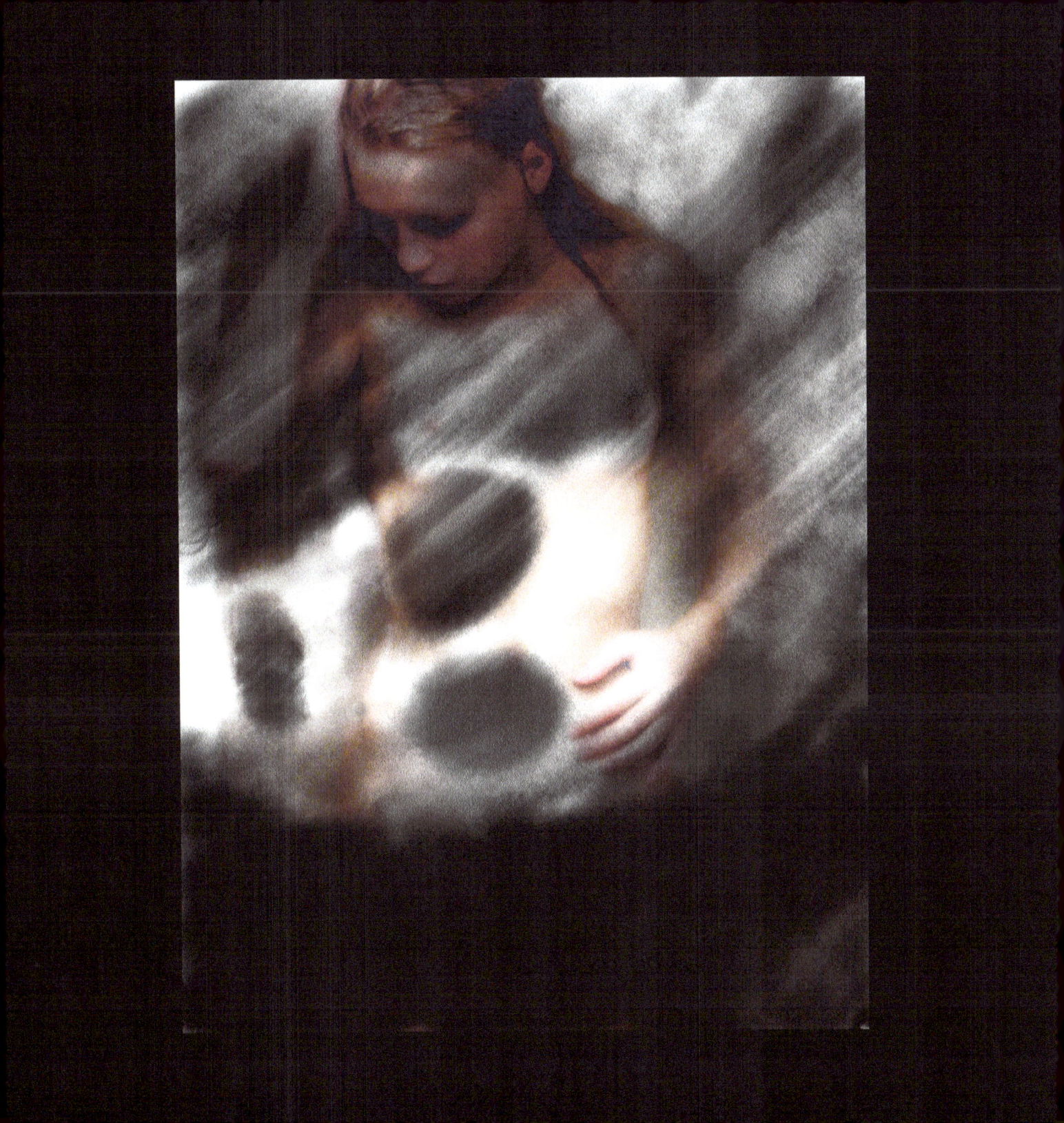

GHOST

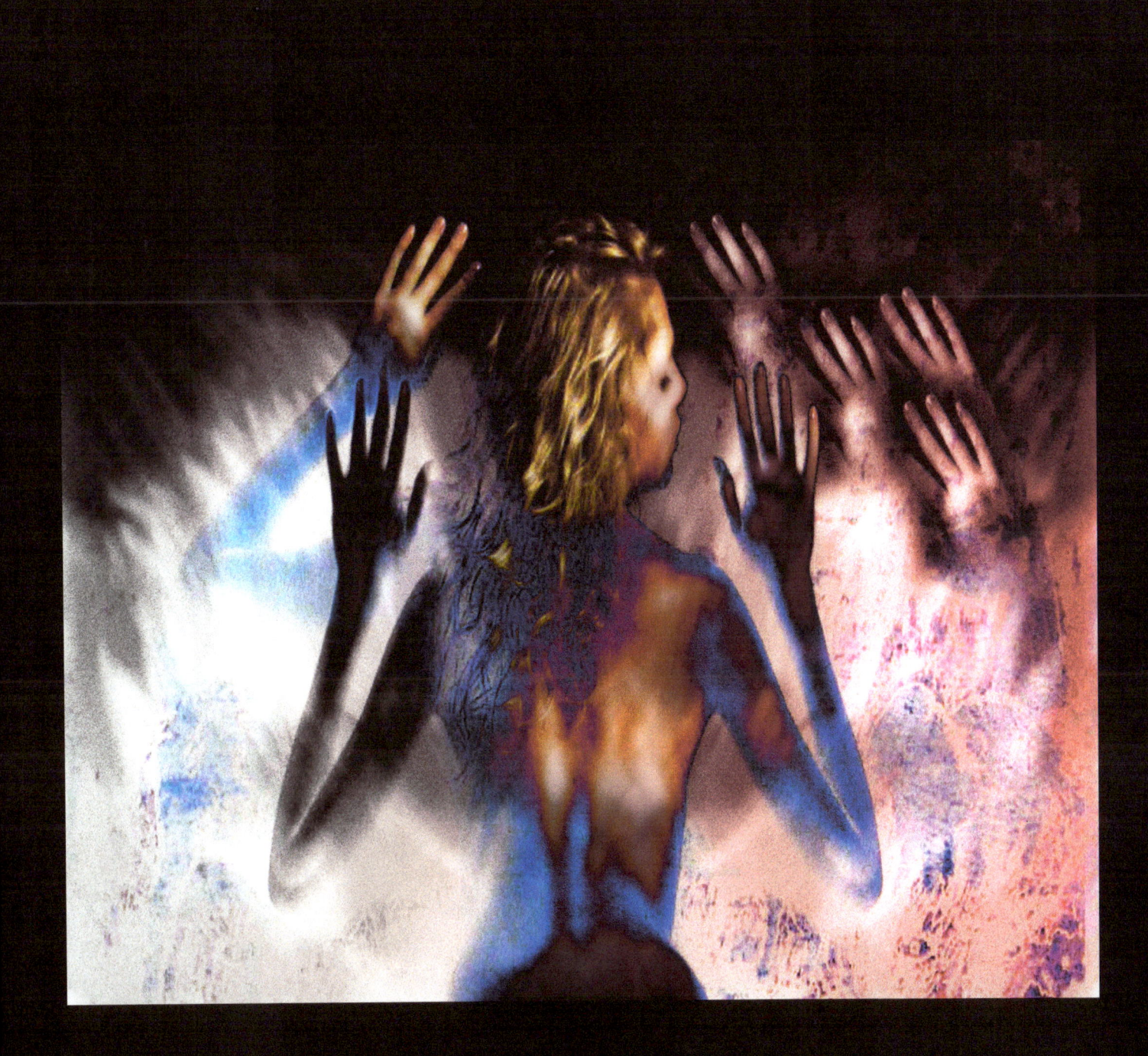

GHOST

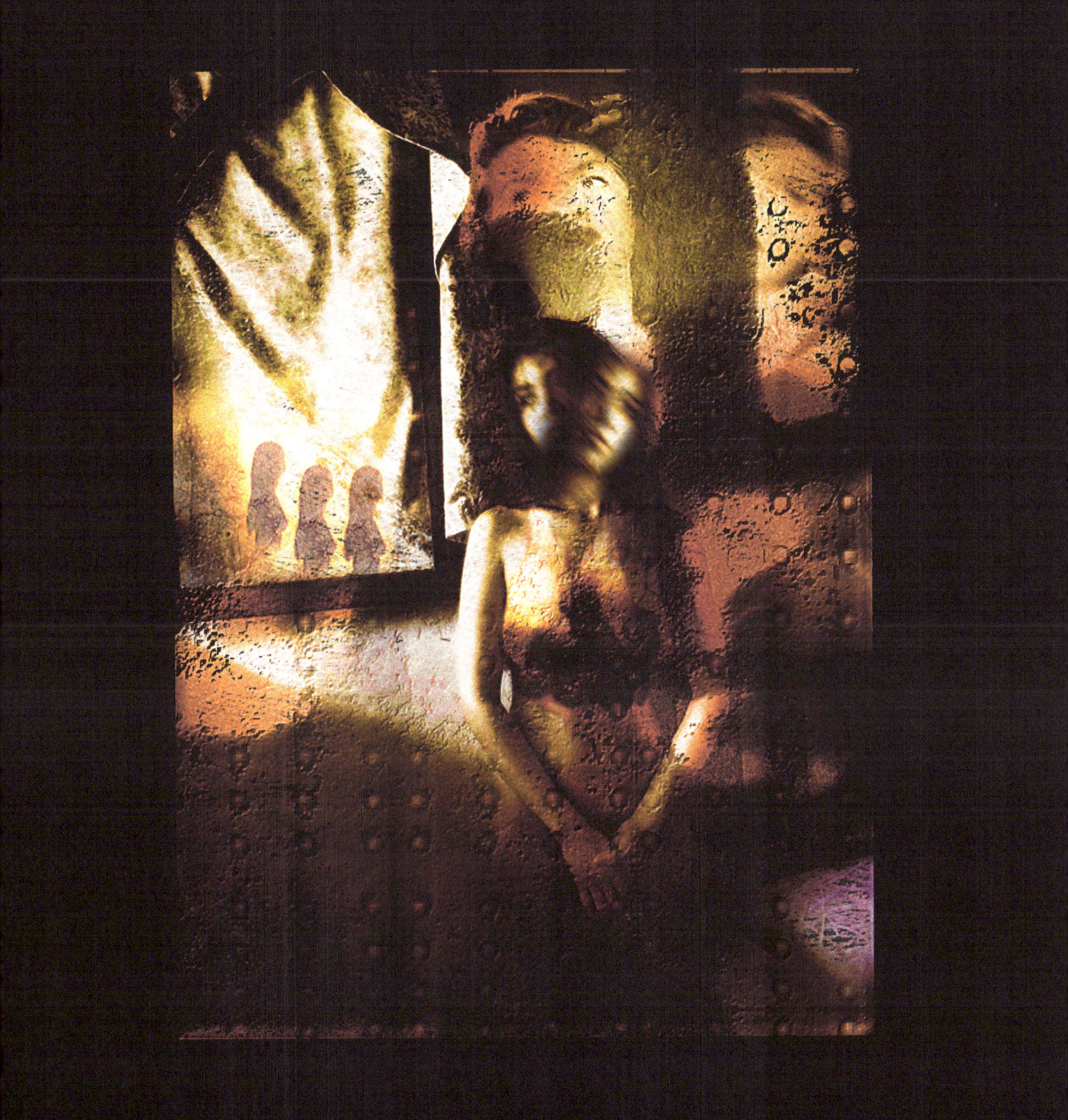

GHOST

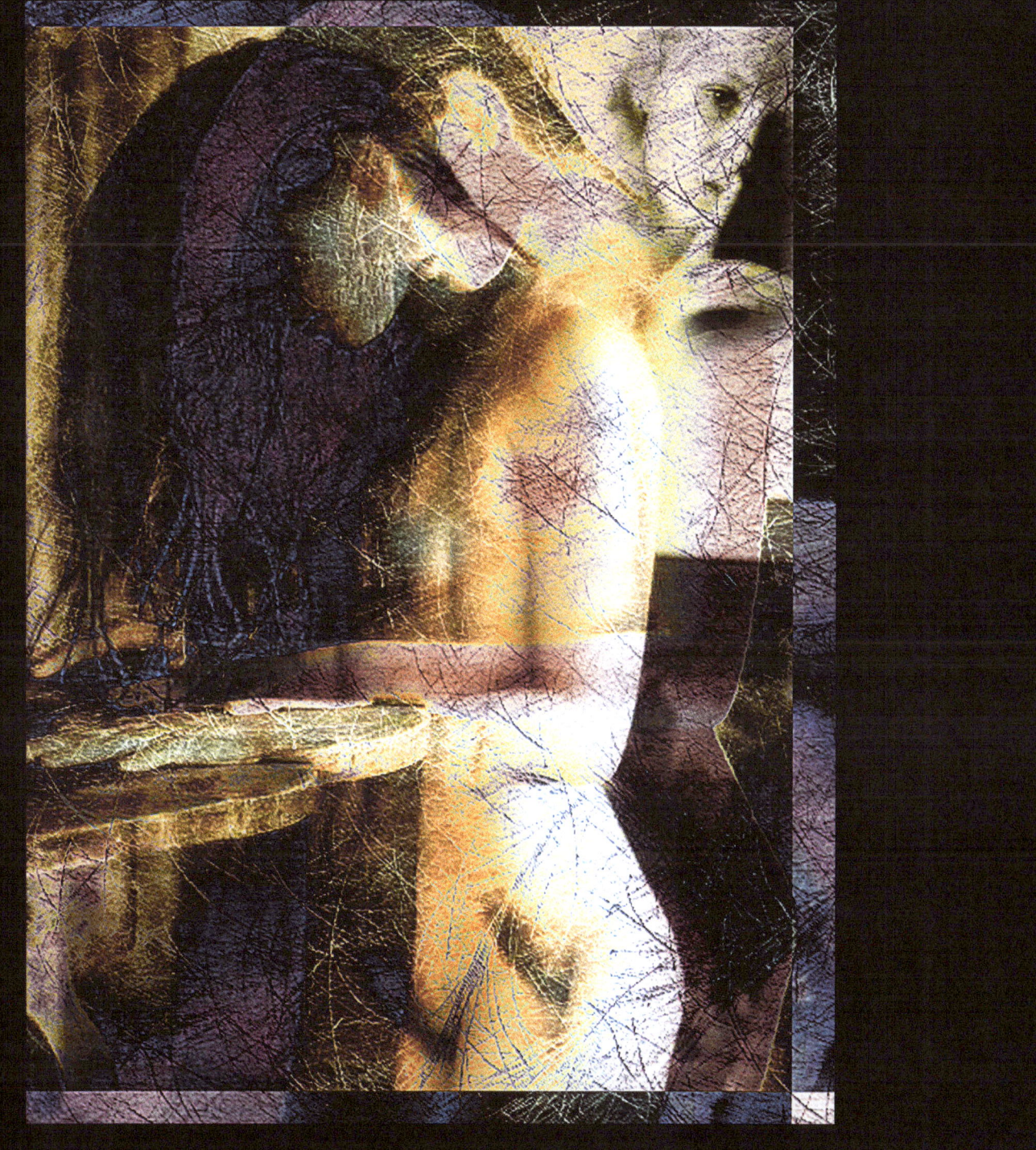

GHOST

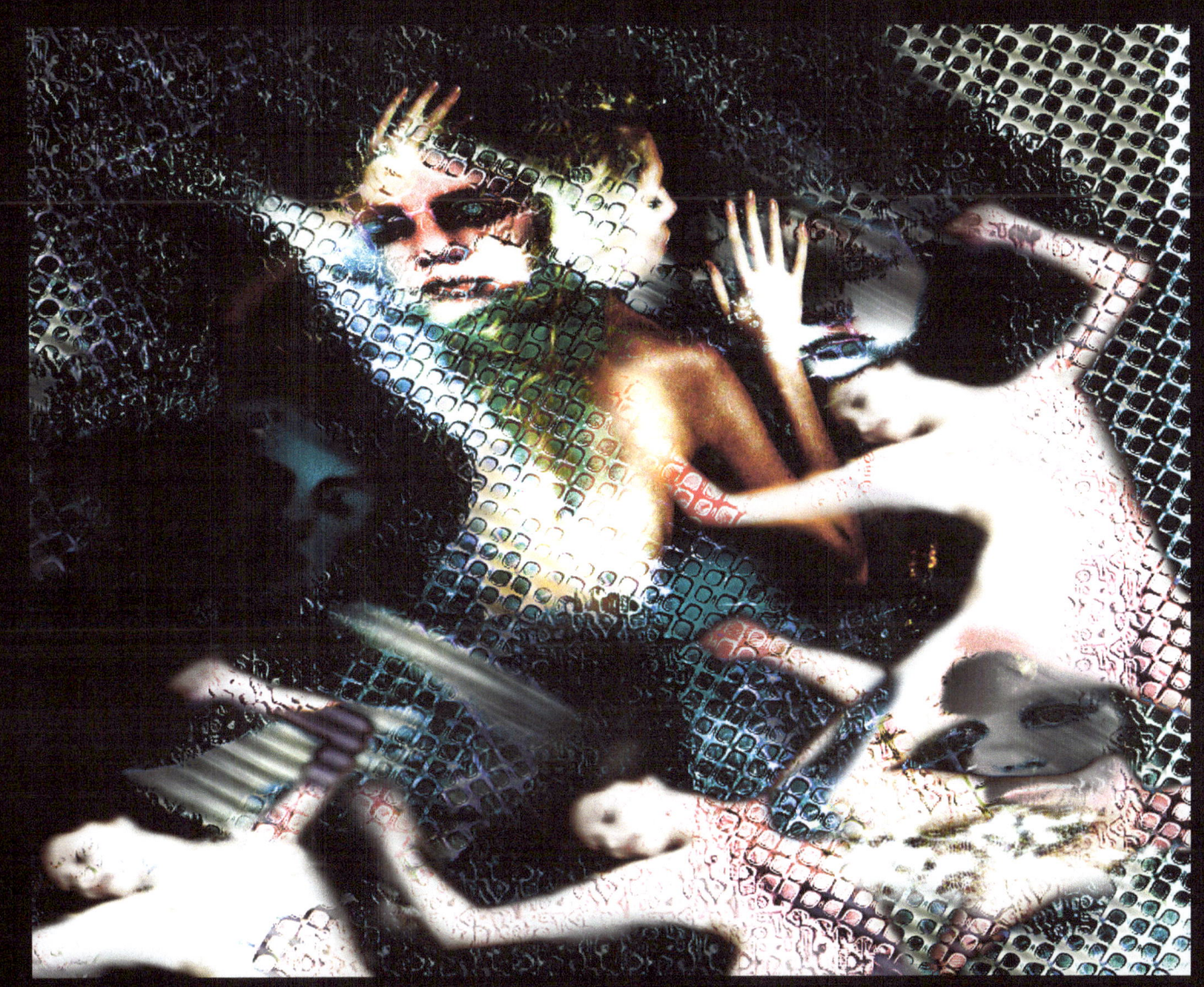

GHOST

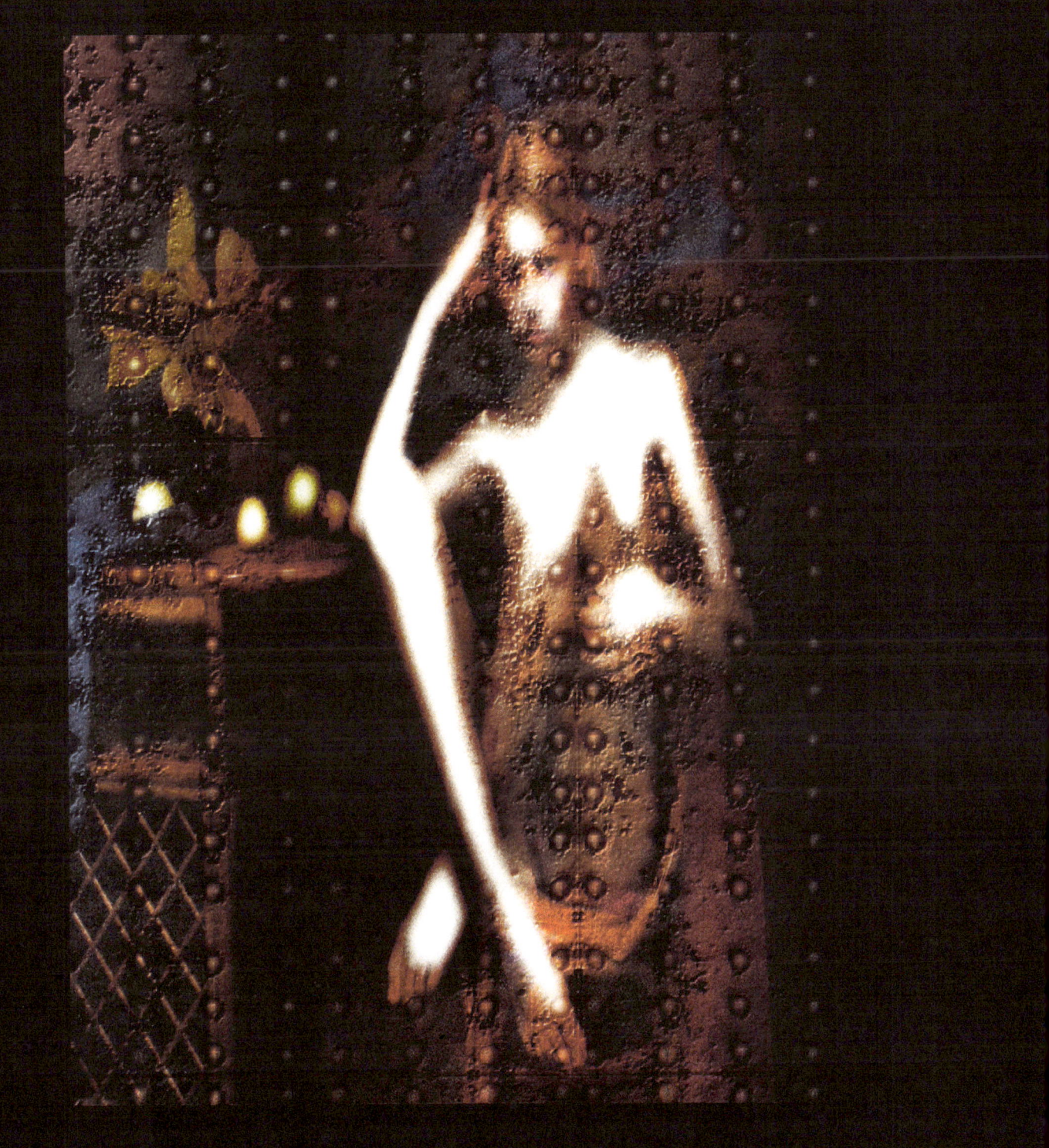

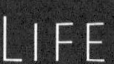

LIFE

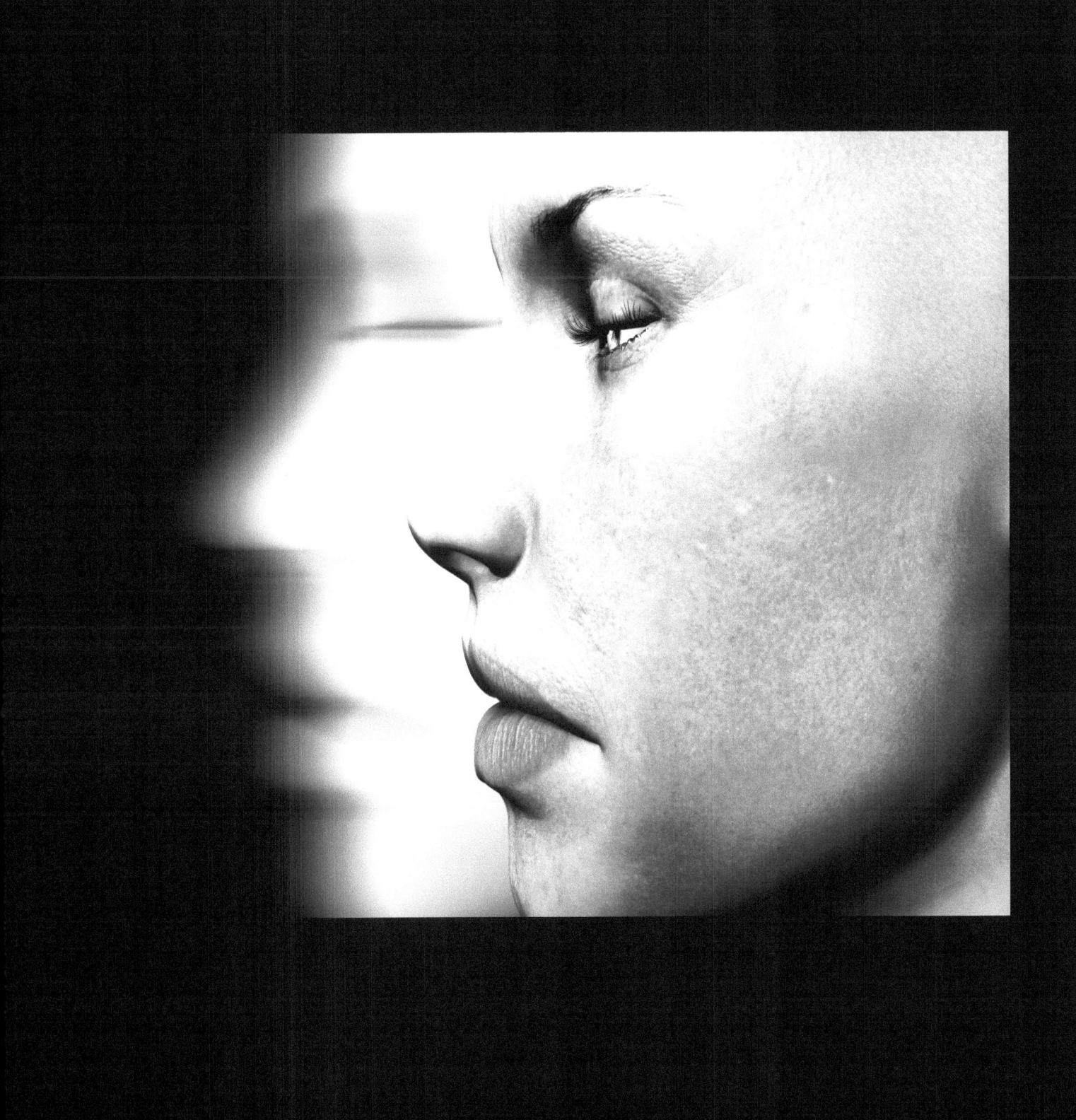

LIFE

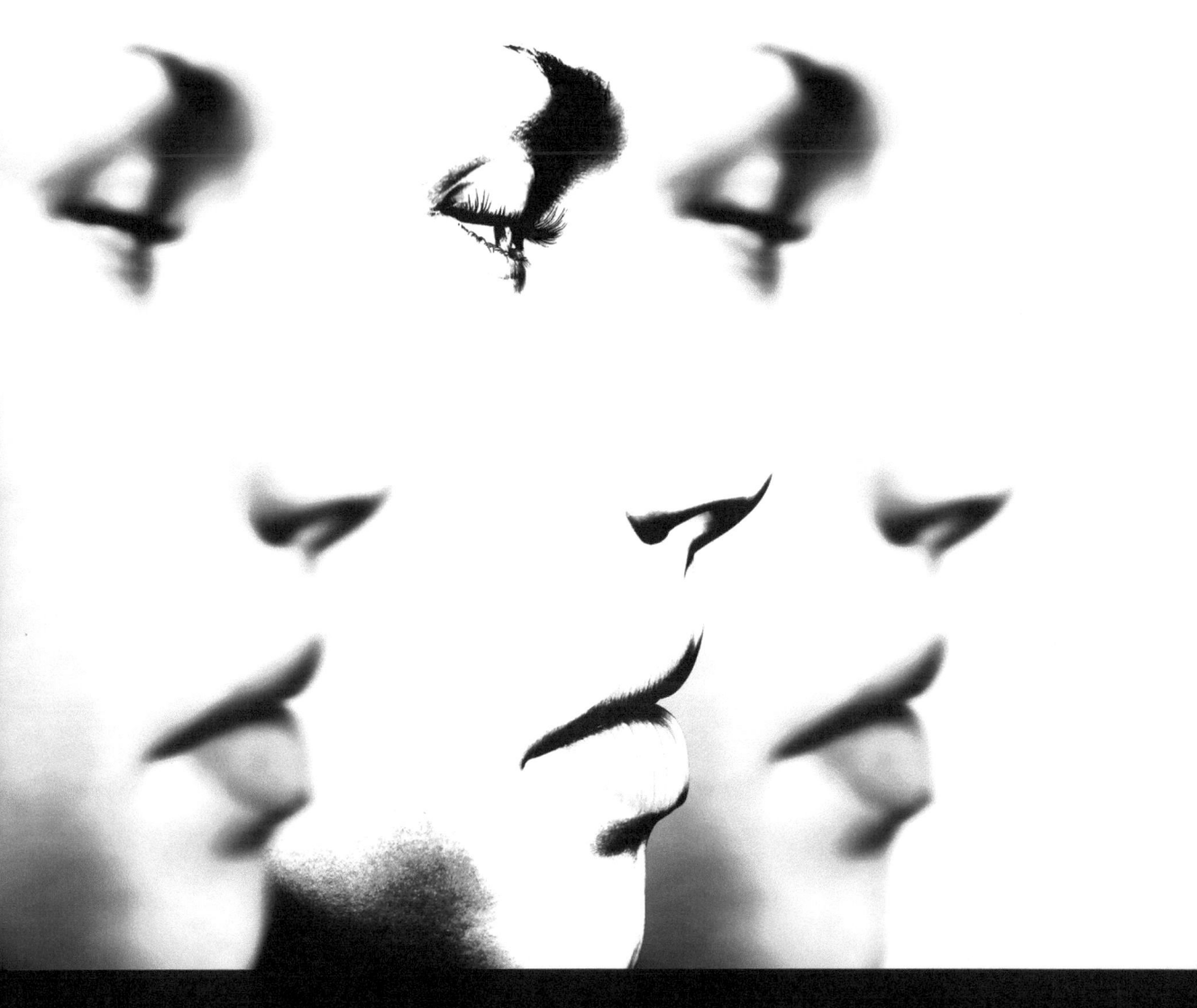

LIFE

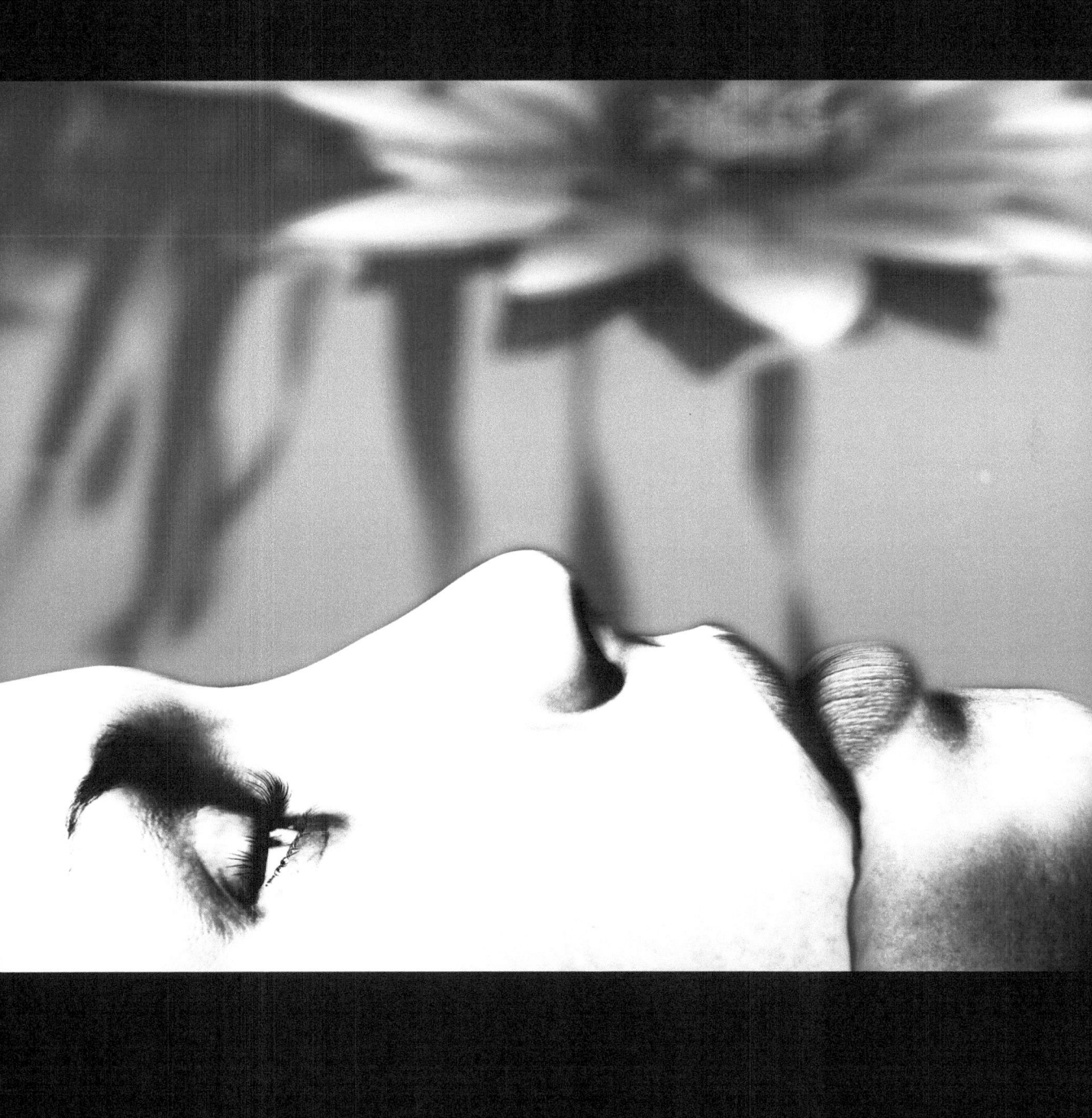

CATS EYE

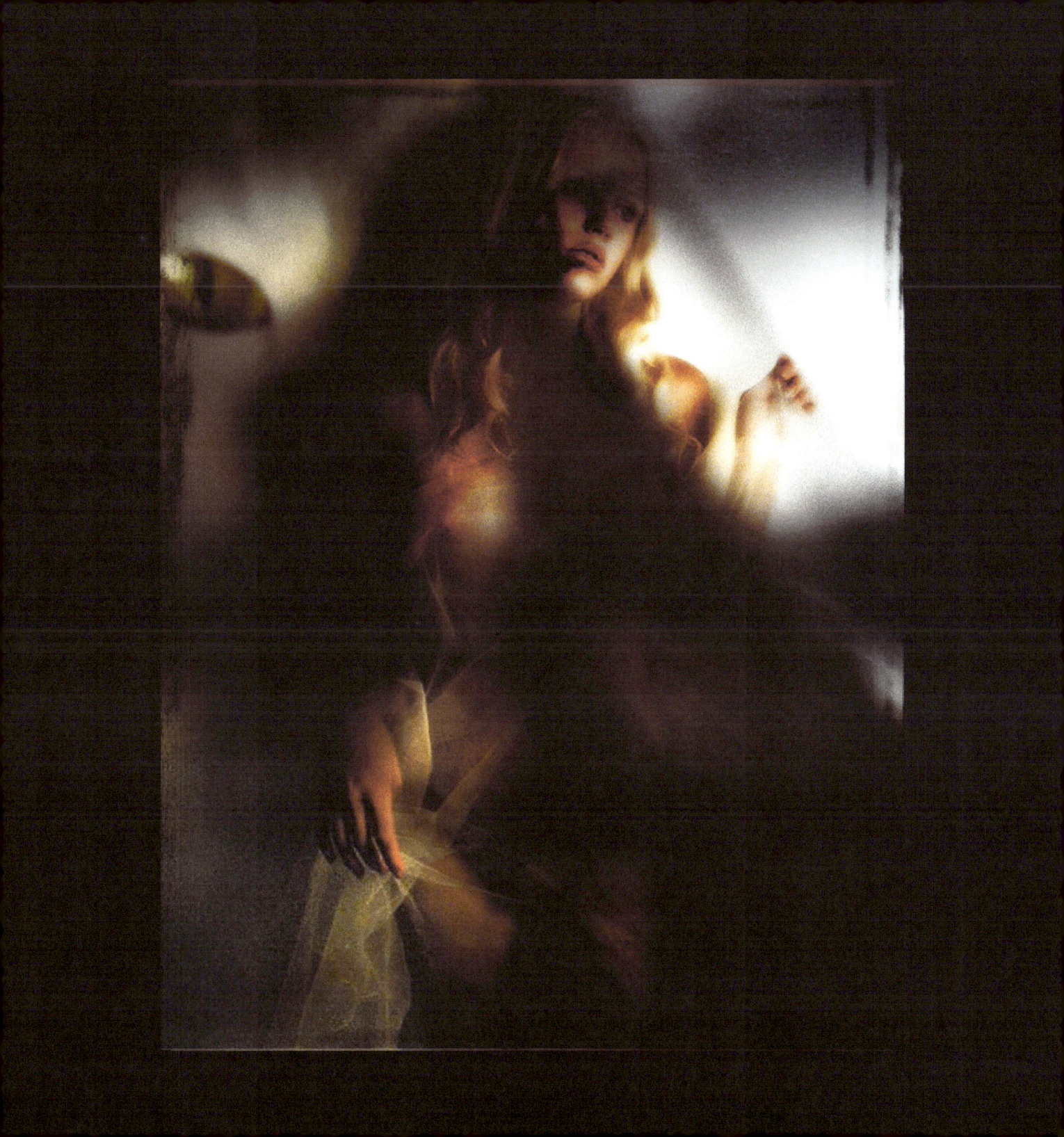

CATS EYE

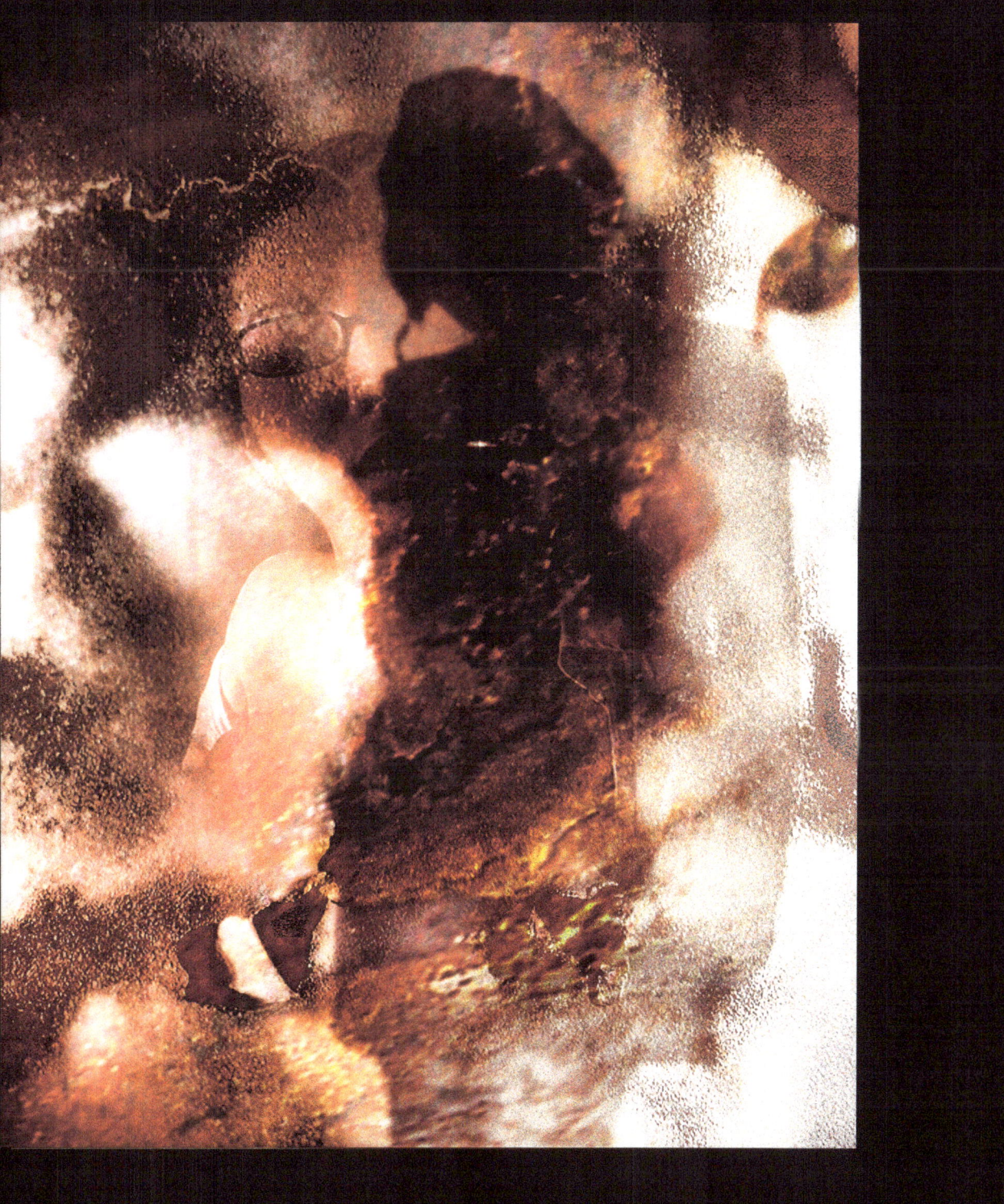

CATS EYE

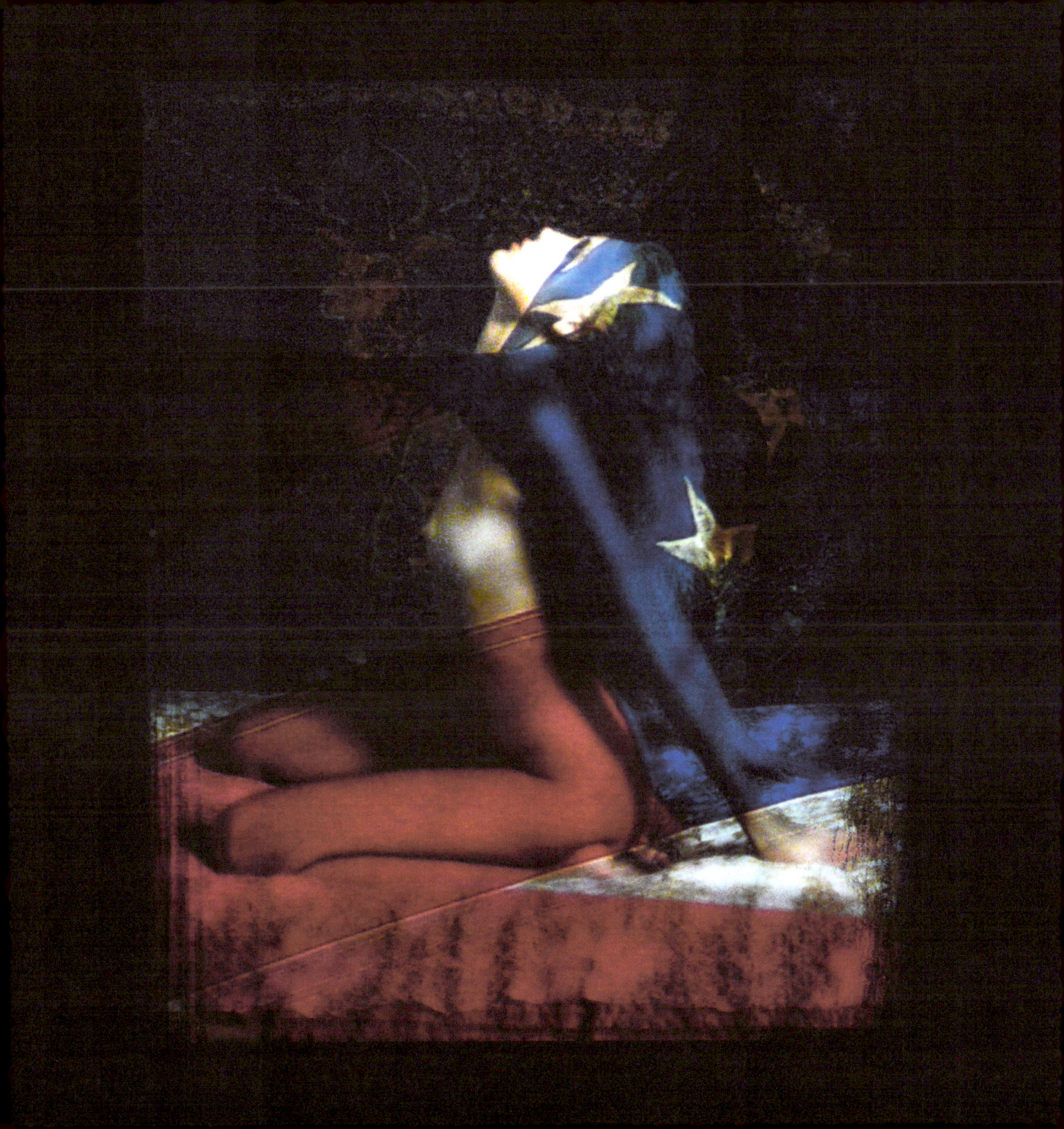

CATS EYE

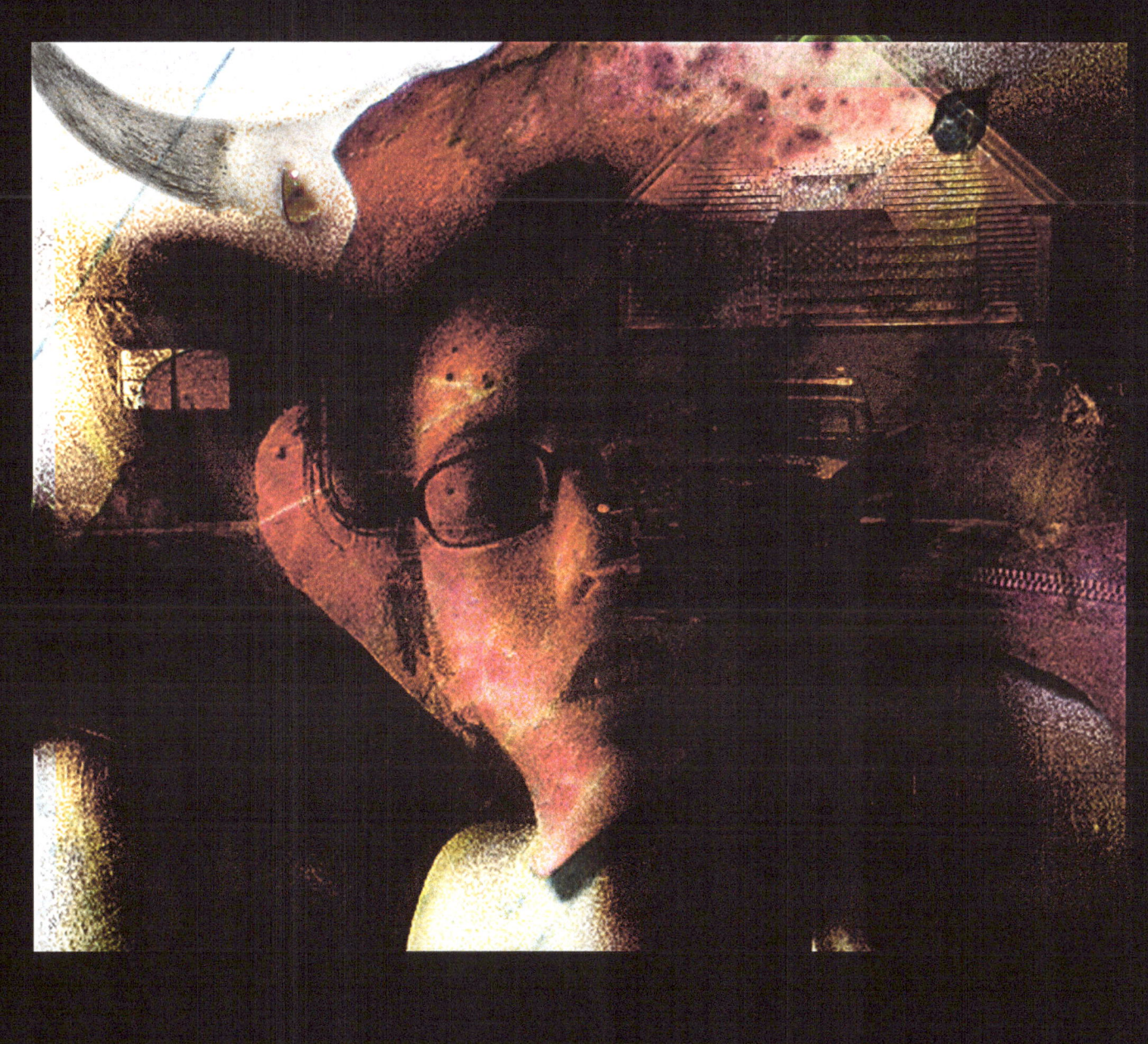

CATS EYE

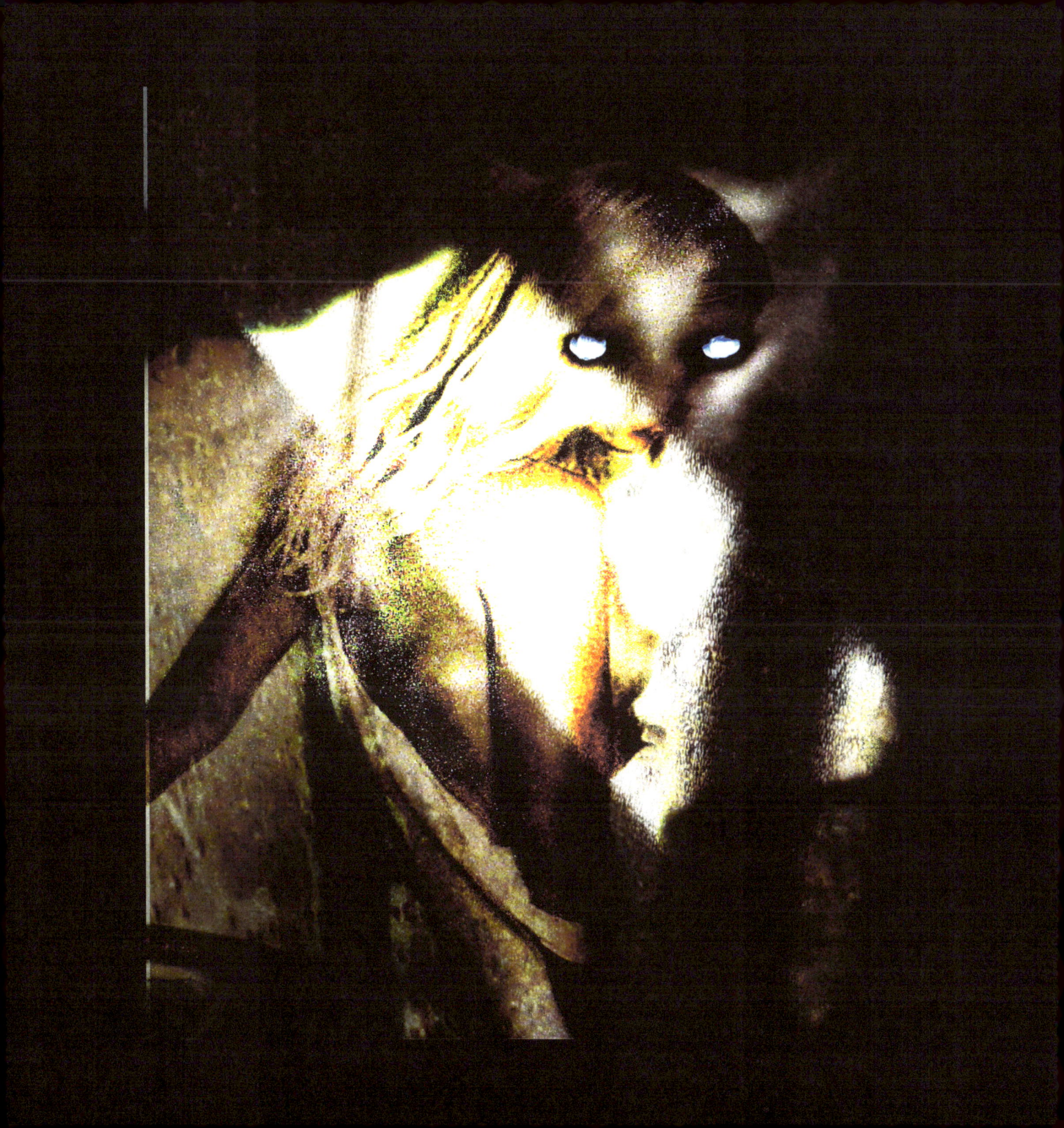

CATS EYE

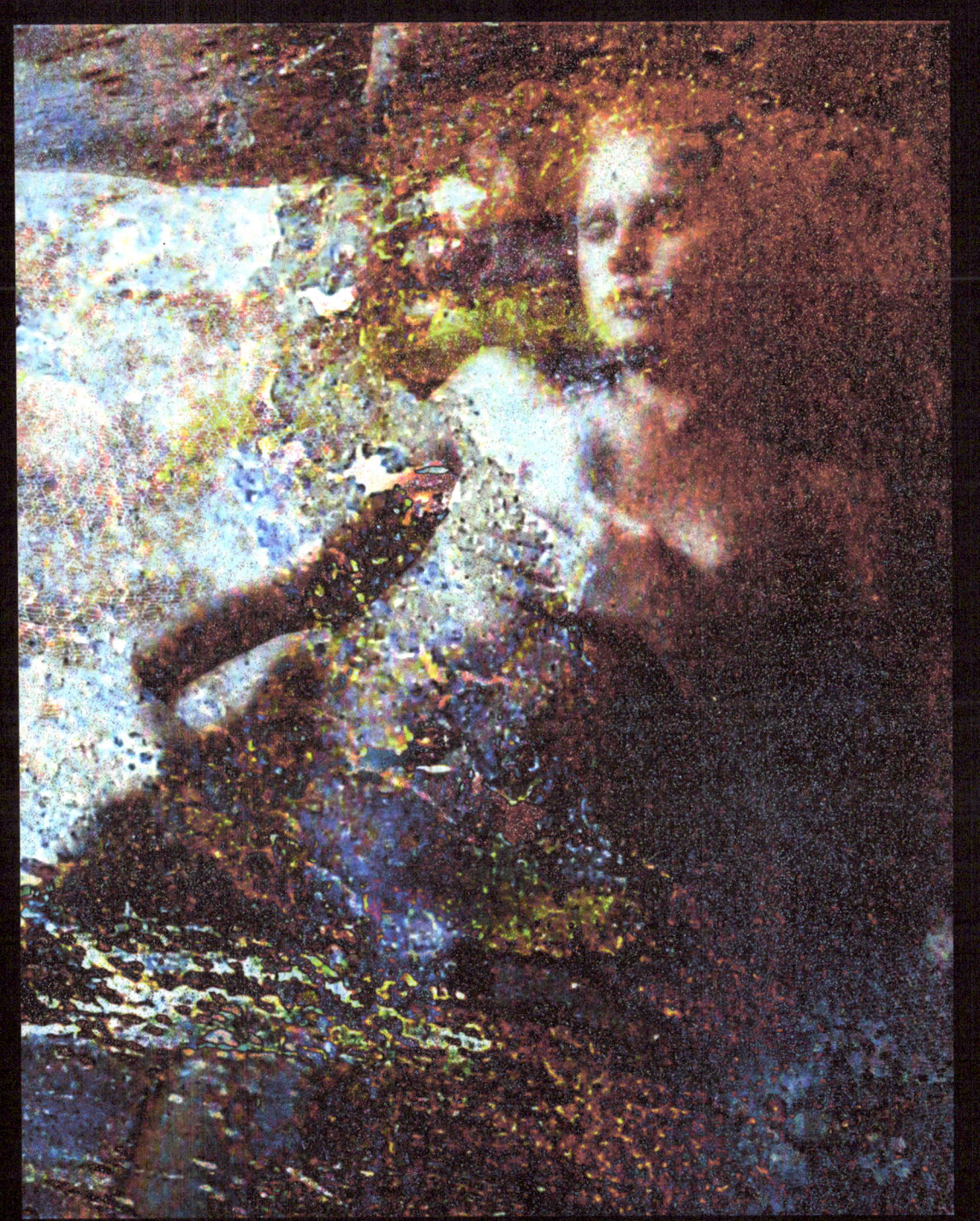

CATS EYE

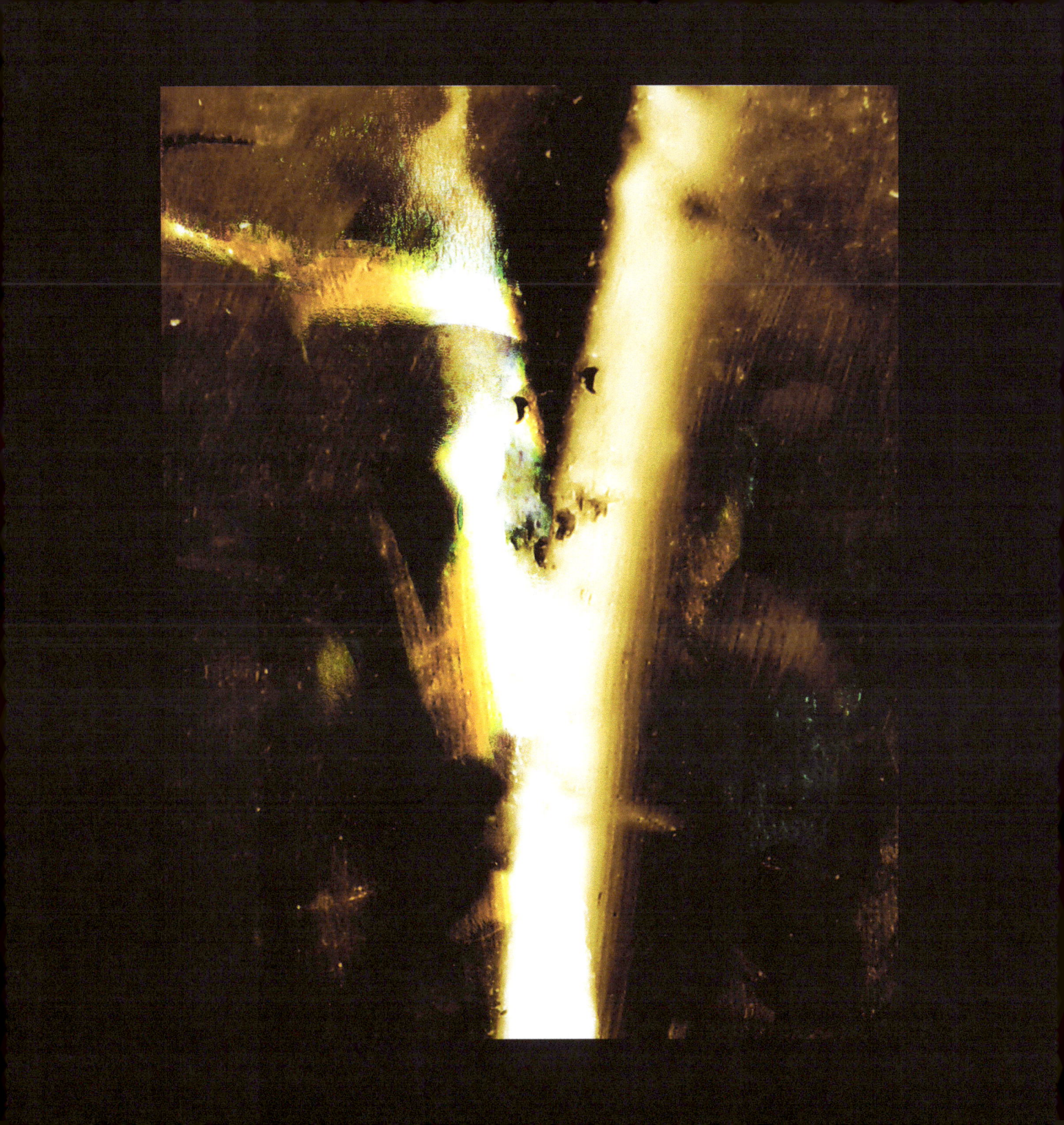

CATS EYE

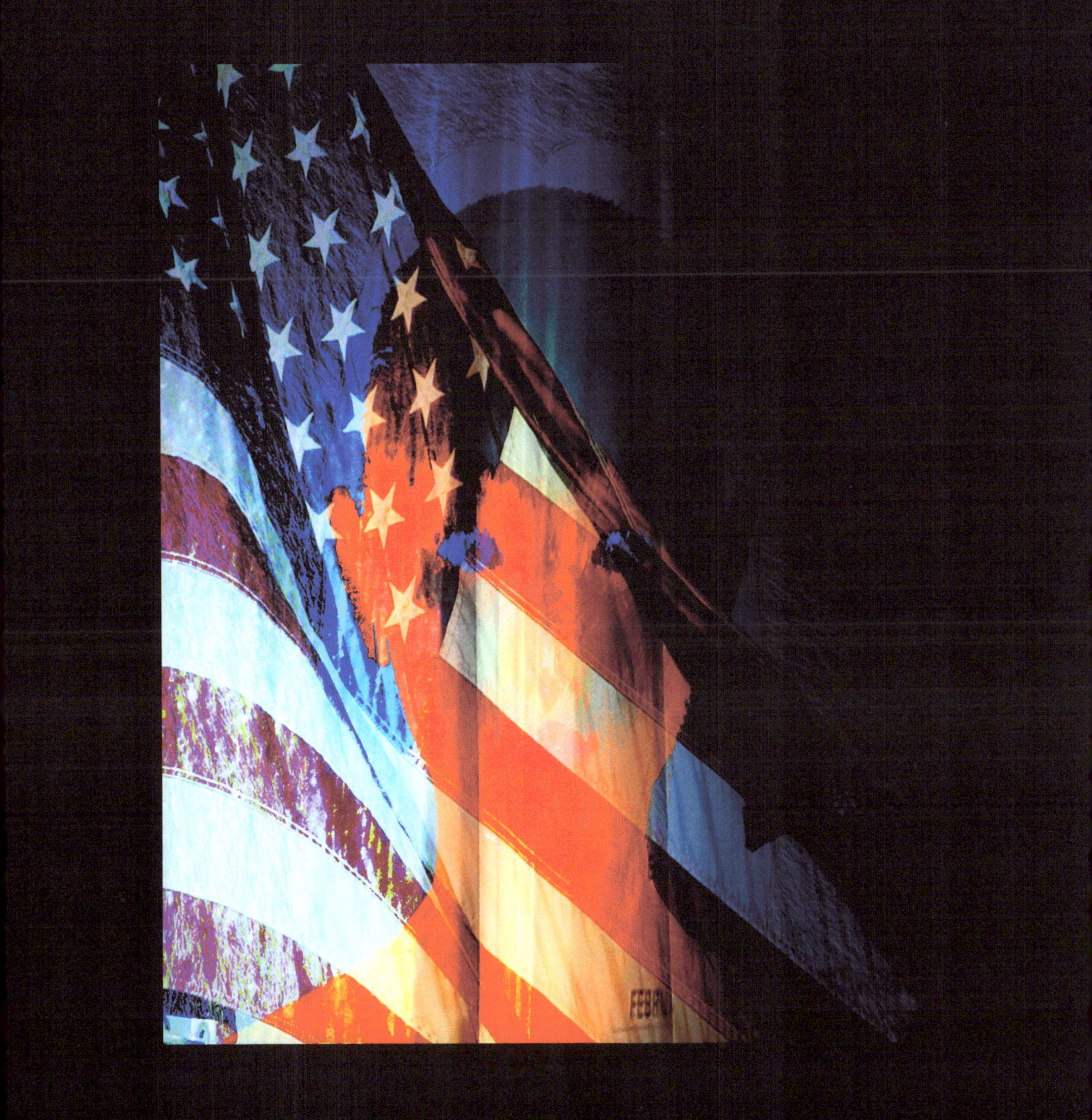

CATS EYE

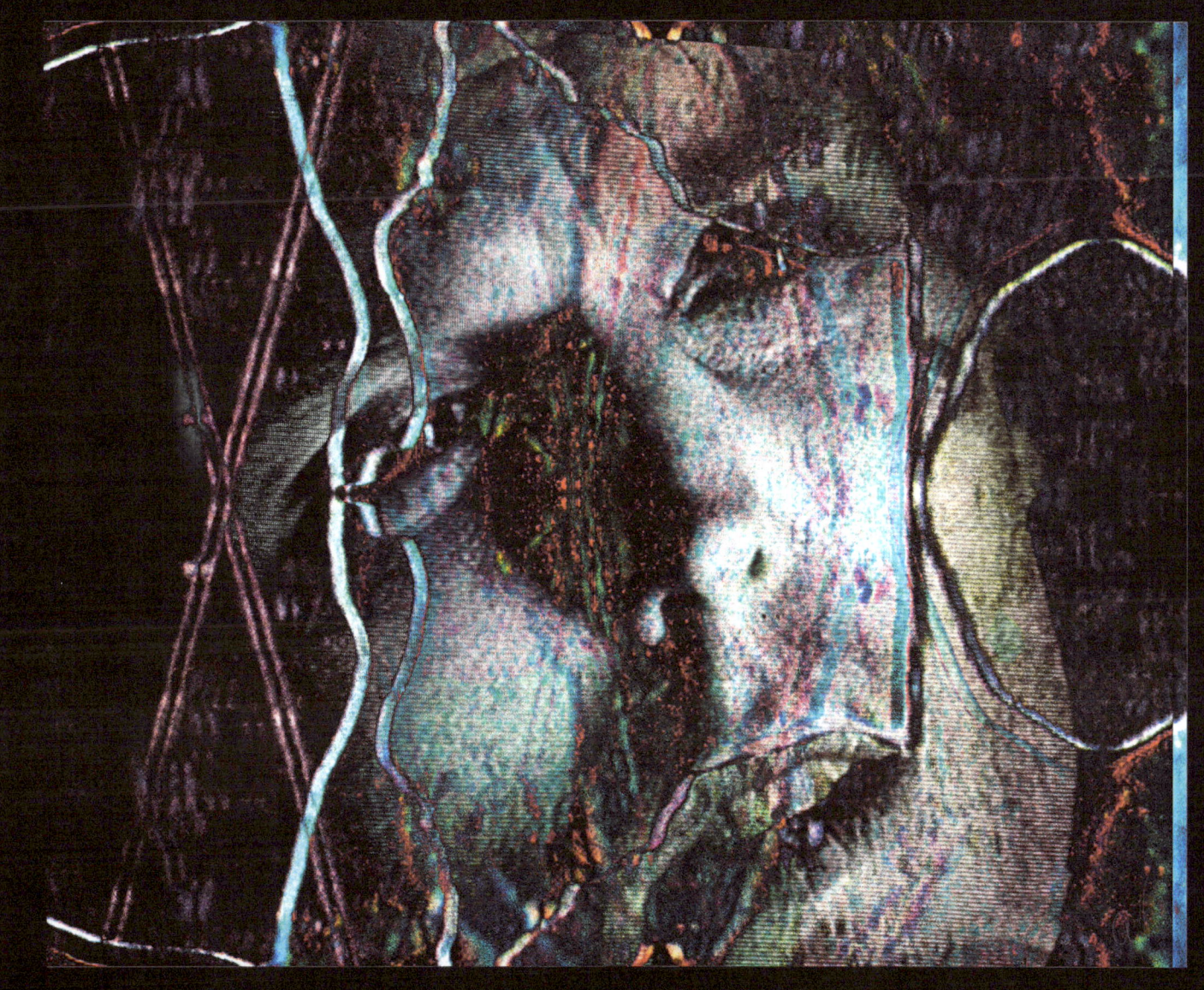

CATS EYE

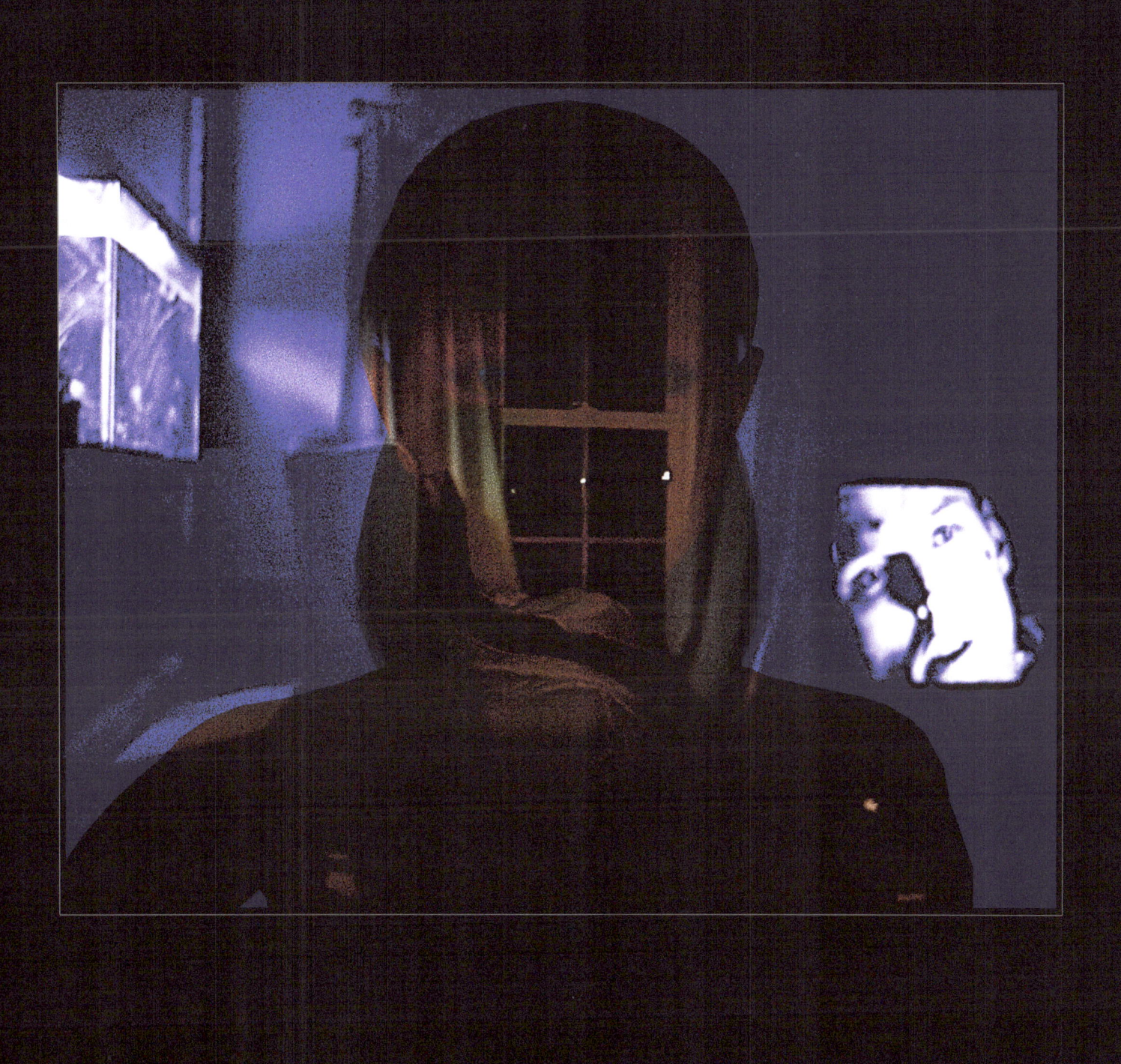

CATS EYE

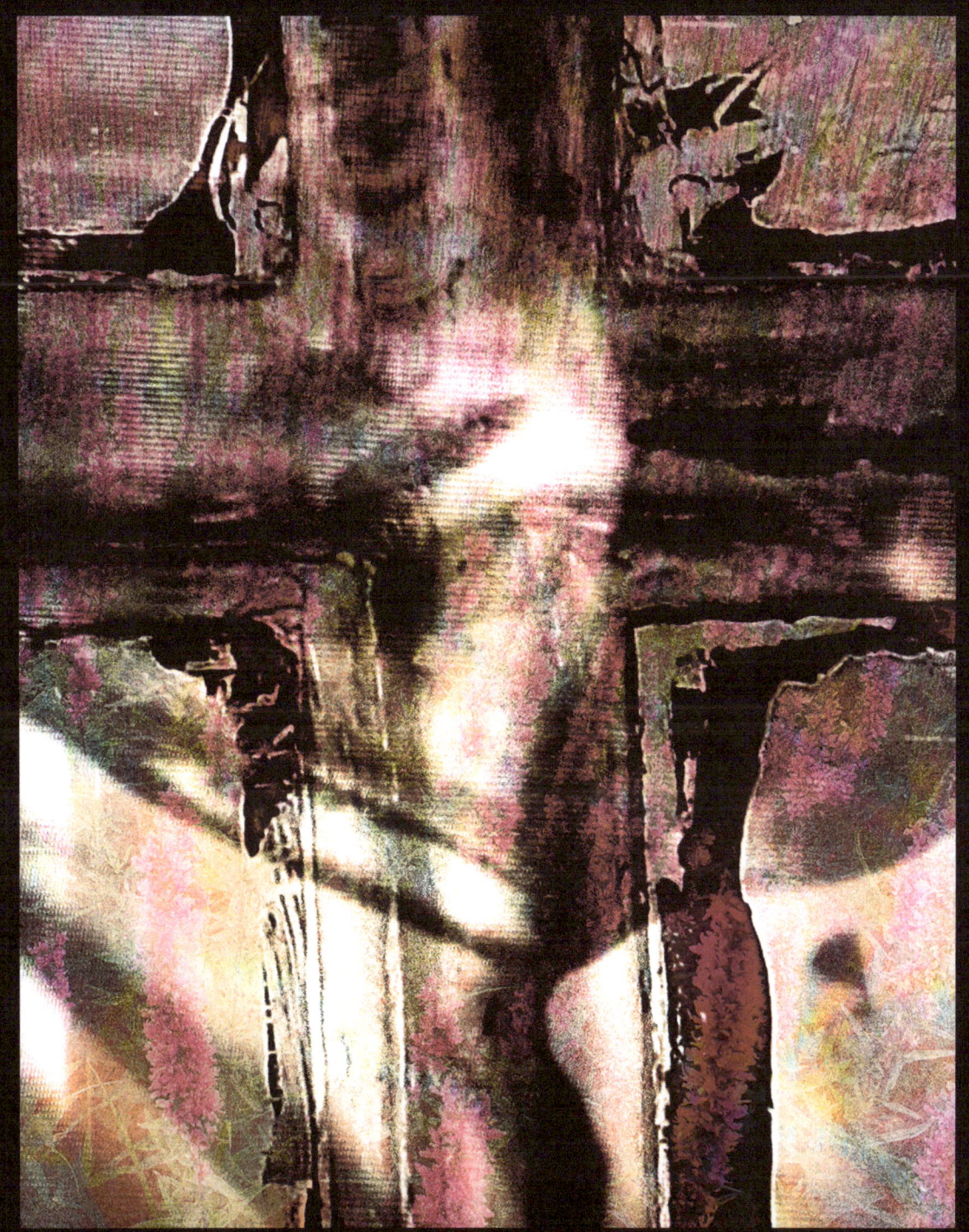

THE SEQUENCE
BY BOB ORSILLO

In the following section each Sequence begins with the actual exhibit catalog cover[1], and then shows the art work grouped as it is displayed on the gallery wall. For this book the art was moved closer together to accommodate the printed page.

_____

[1] The exhibit catalog usually consists of a list of art work currently on display in the gallery, along with reproductions and the provenance of each work. If the art is for sale, the prices may also be listed.

Depending on the exhibit or show, the catalog is produced by the gallery with copies sent to gallery patrons. Copies are also made available to visitors to the exhibit. Artists sometimes produce their own catalog to be sent to patrons who collect their art.

GHOST

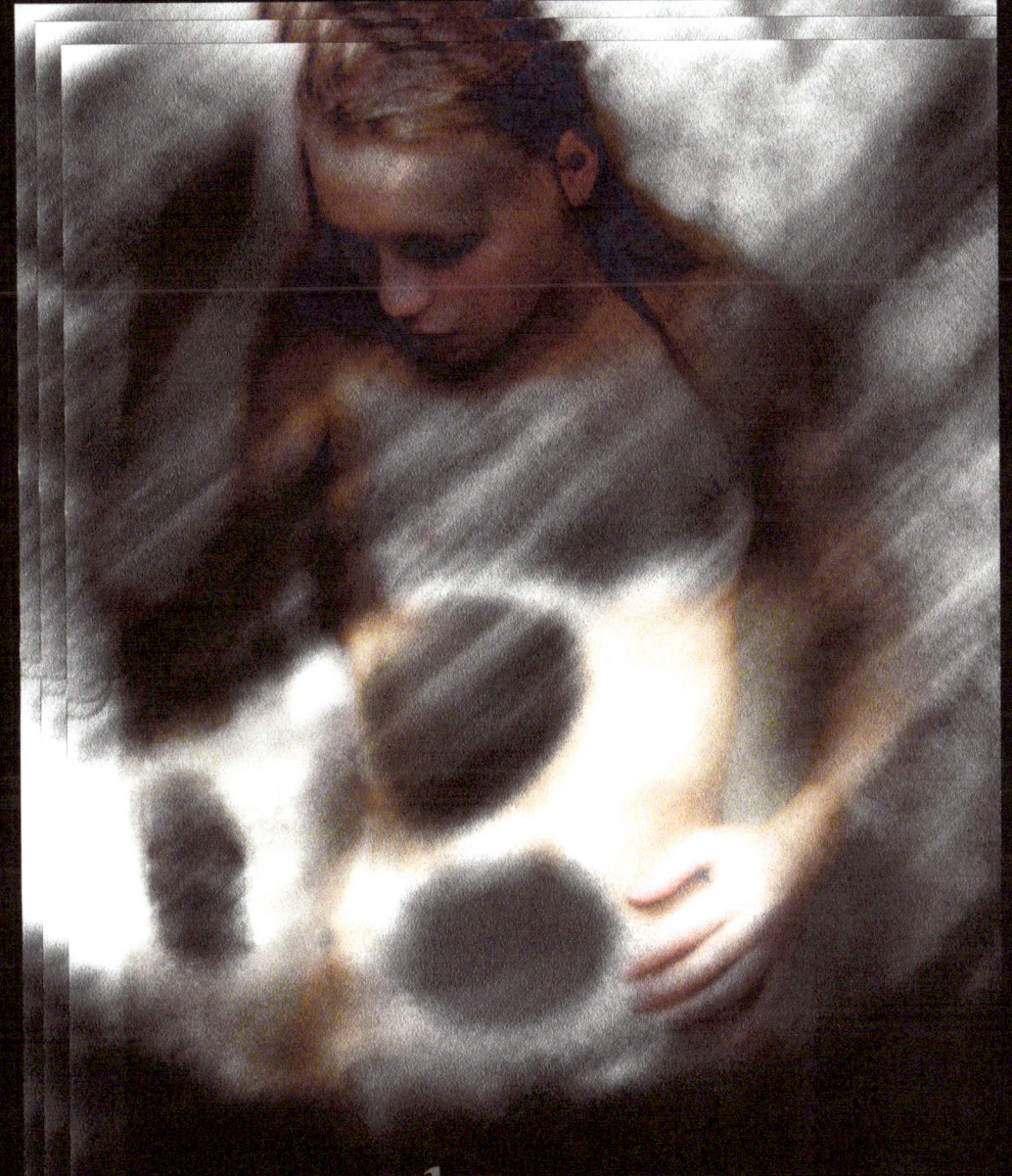

Ghost Sequence

Ghost Sequence

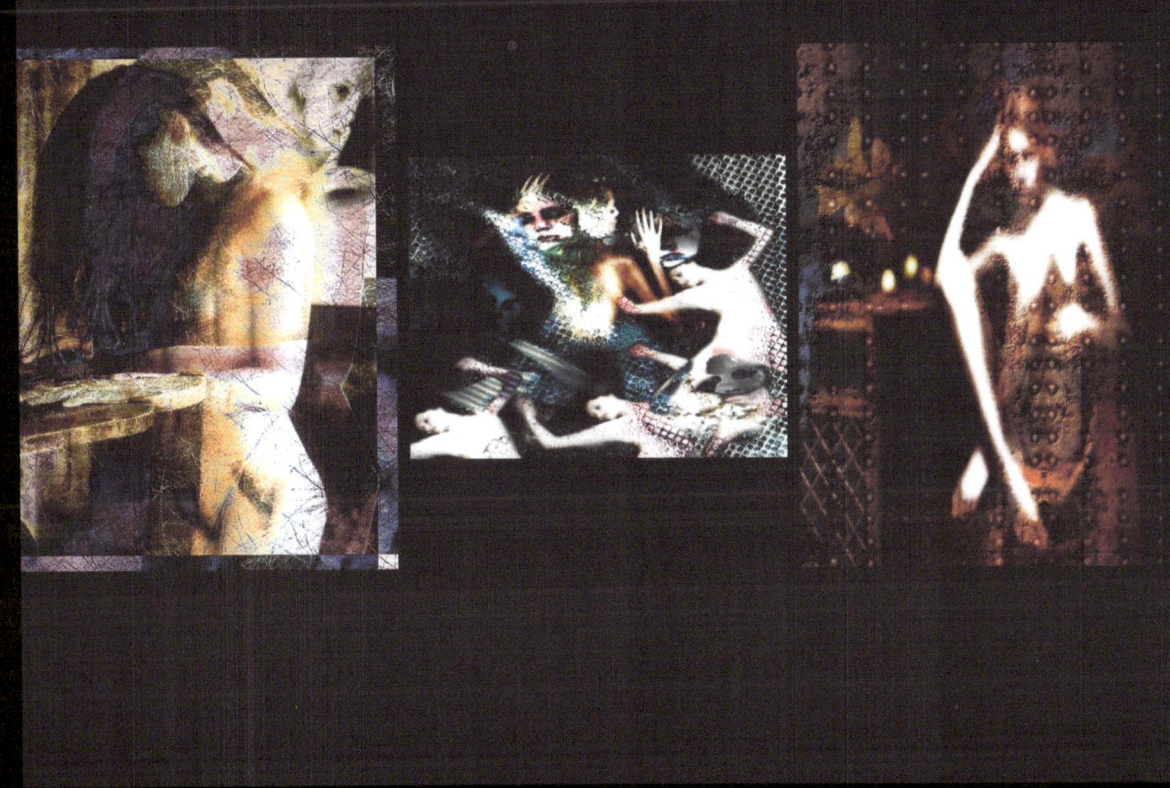

LIFE

Life Sequence

Life Sequence

CATS EYE

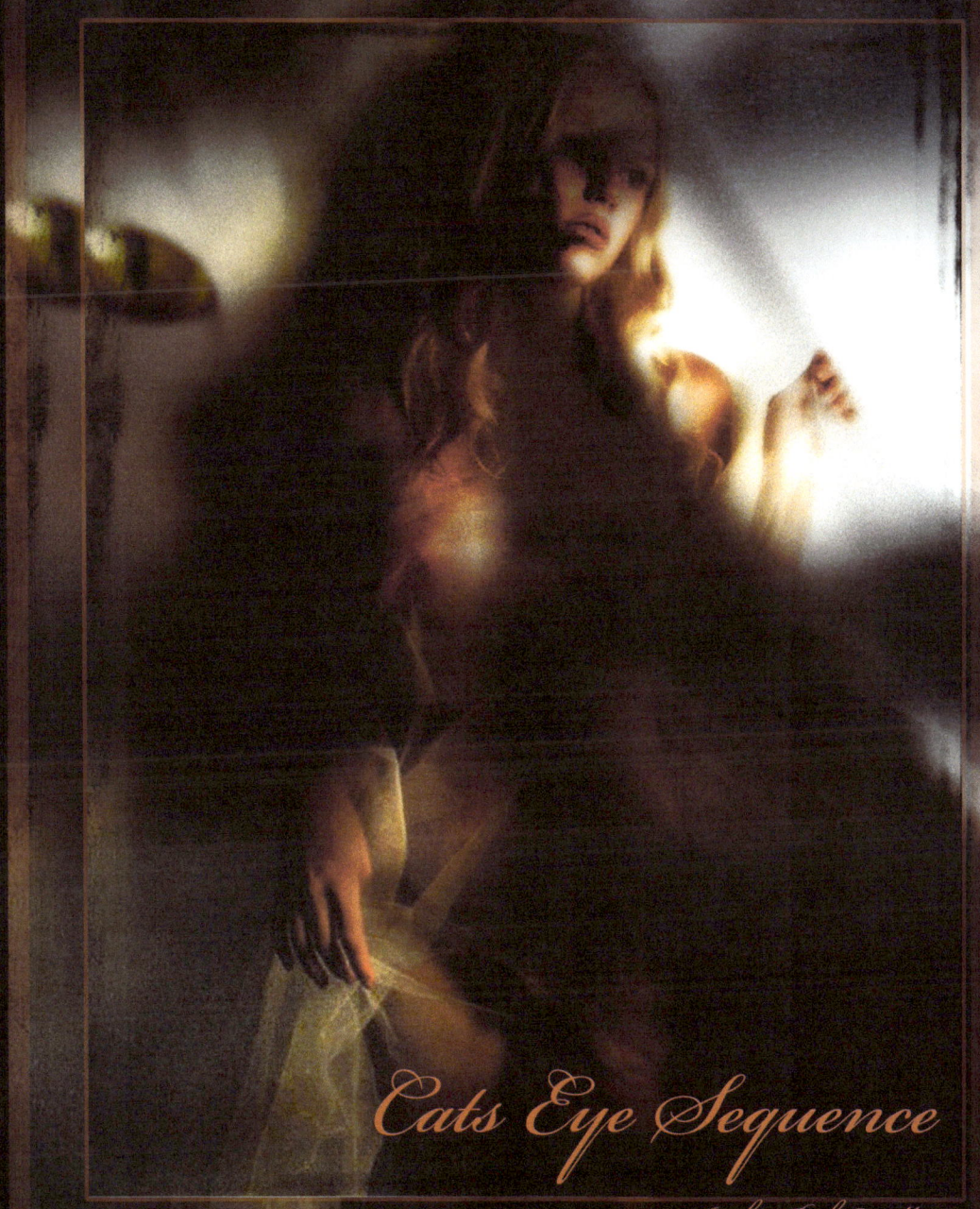

Cats Eye Sequence

Art by Bob Orsillo

Cats Eye Sequence

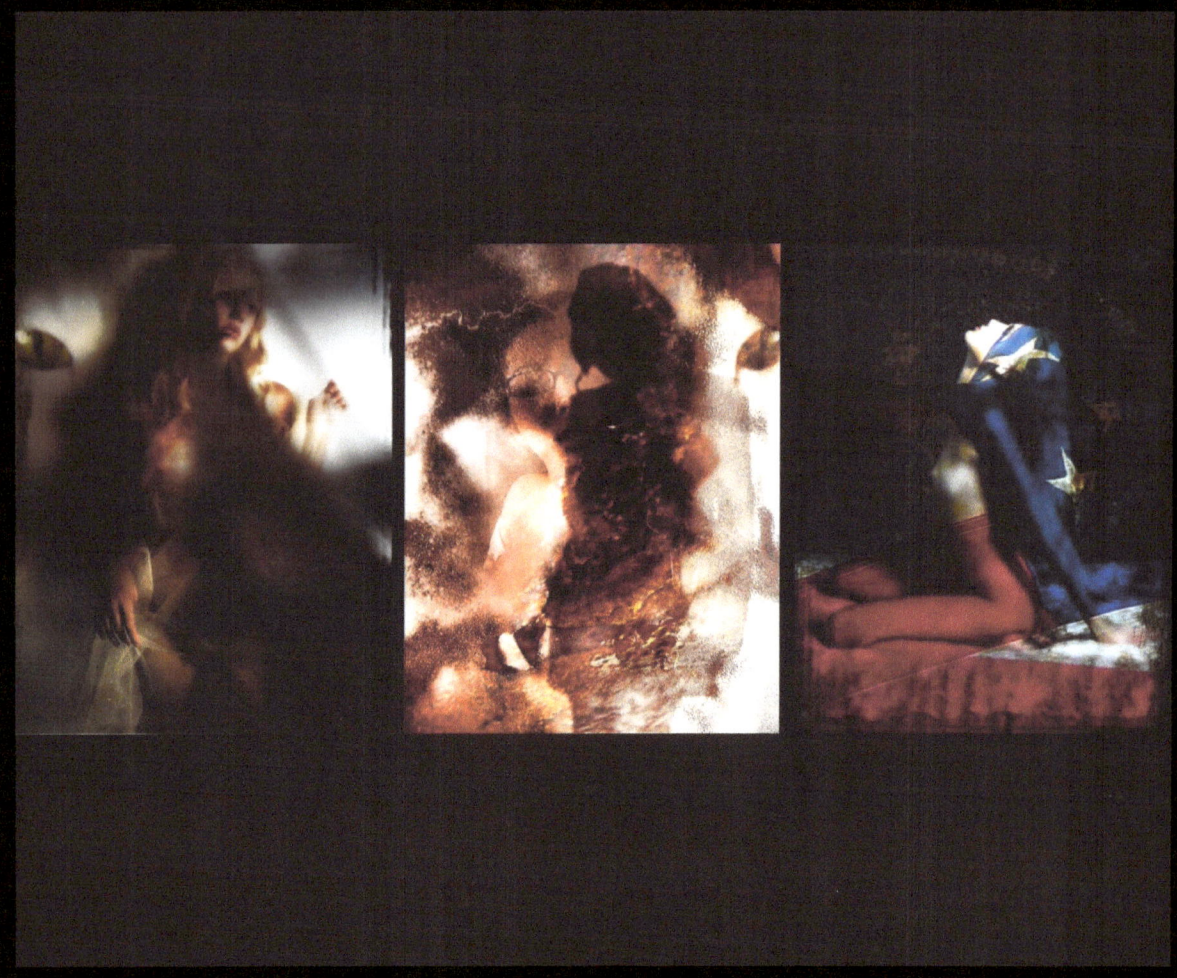

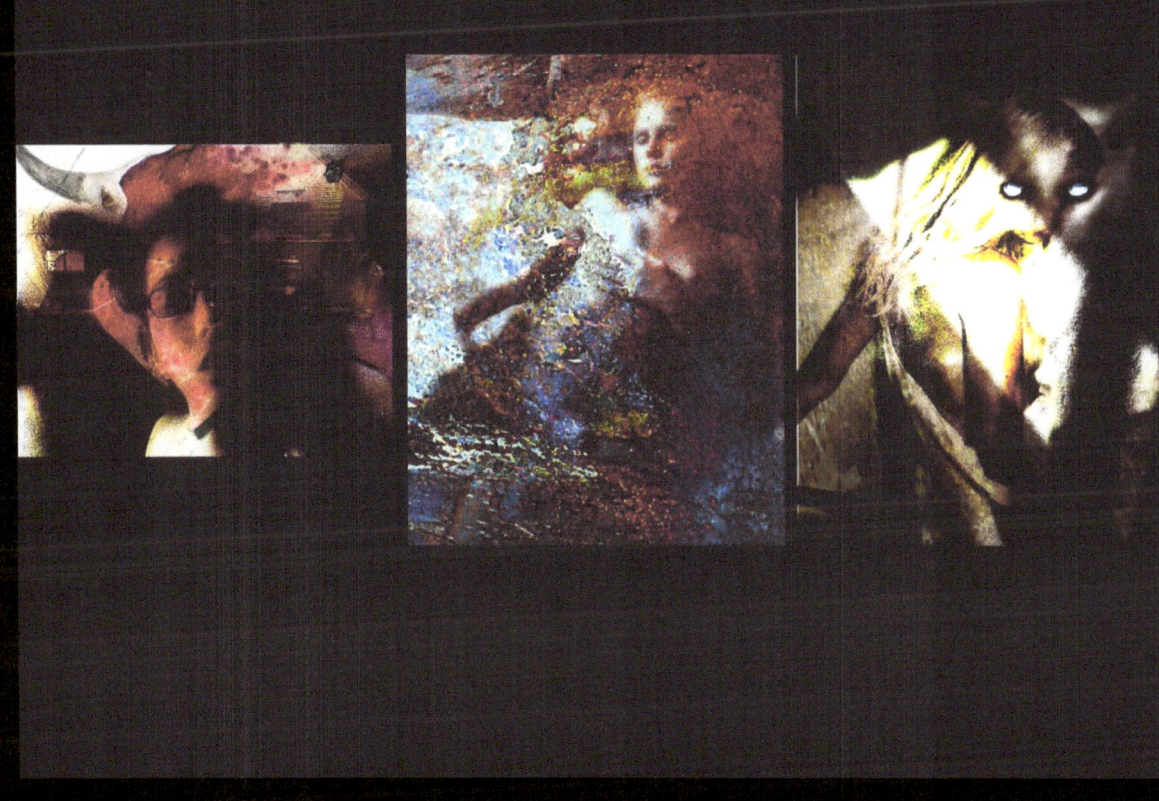

Cats Eye Sequence

Bob Orsillo

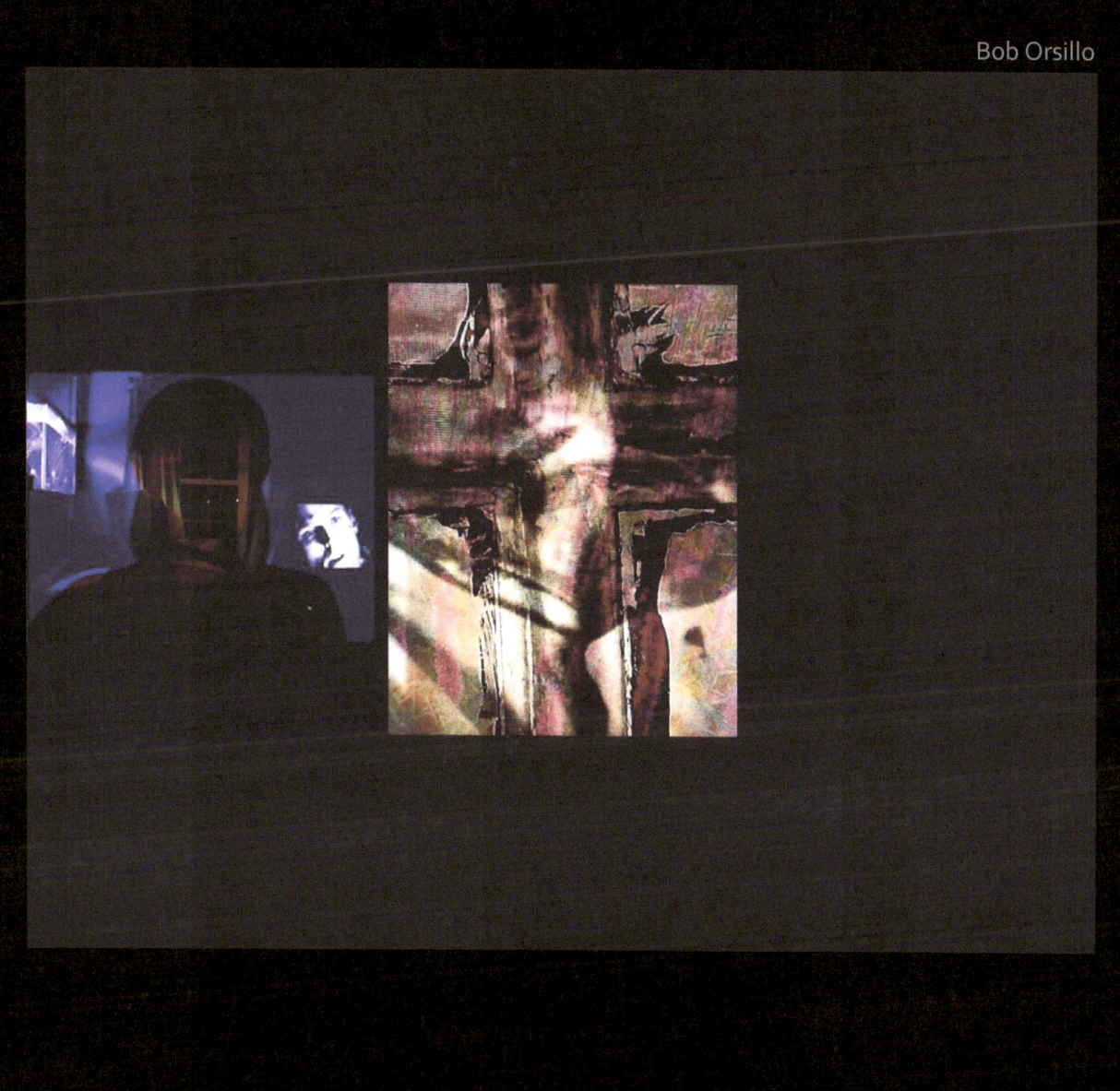

THE SEQUENCE

BY BOB ORSILLO

About The Artist:

A Multiple Media artist; Bob Orsillo's art work is as diverse as the materials he uses. For over four decades he has worked to master both the craft and the art. In doing so he is honored with many prestigious national and international awards for his paintings, photography and sculpture. Since the 1970's he has shared his vision in over two thousand exhibits worldwide.

Bob Orsillo's art work is highly collected by galleries, museums, public and private corporations and individuals on five continents. In addition you can see Bob's art in major motion pictures, television, book and magazine covers, record albums and CD covers. And if you were in New England in the late 60's and early 70's you may have seen his wall murals that covered entire factory buildings or his massive industrial sculptures.

He is called one of the most important Multiple Media artists alive today. "America's best kept secret", "a combination of Edgar Allen Poe and William Shakespeare, but in good way", and "For those who care to look, Orsillo's art work is a visual journey to familiar places we have never been" are a few of the descriptive phases attributed to Bob Orsillo and his artwork.

"The process is the pleasure, the results are the passion".
Bob Orsillo - *published September 2007 " In The Studio"*

---

[i] *Multiple Media Artist:
An Artist that does not work in one specific medium, but chooses the medium that best suits their personal vision.

www.ingramcontent.com/pod-product-compliance
Lightning Source LLC
Chambersburg PA
CBHW051026180526
45172CB00002B/481